EXPERIENCING GOD DIRECTLY

The Way Of Christian Nonduality

MARSHALL DAVIS

I make it my business only to persevere in His holy Presence, wherein I keep myself by a simple attention, and a general fond regard to GOD, which I may call an actual presence of GOD; or, to speak better, an habitual, silent and secret conversation of the soul with GOD, which often causes me joys and raptures inwardly, and sometimes also outwardly, so great, that I am forced to use means to moderate them and prevent their appearance to others. In short, I am assured beyond all doubt that my soul has been with GOD above these thirty years.

- Brother Lawrence of the Resurrection (1614 – 1691)
The Practice of the Presence of God

.

CONTENTS

Introduction - What is Nondual Christianity?   1

1   Jesus as a Proclaimer of Nonduality   12

2   UnBorn Again   24

3   Self-Inquiry   34

4   God Inquiry   49

5   The Power of Negative Thinking   62

6   The Wayless Way   73

Epilogue - The Story of Me   87

INTRODUCTION

What is Nondual Christianity?

This book is about experiencing God directly. It is not meant to give the reader new spiritual insights or a better understanding of God. It is not trying to communicate theological knowledge about God gleaned from Scripture and expressed in ideas and concepts. It is not about designing a worship service with the right mix of music, words, and symbolism in order to prompt a religious experience of God. It is not about achieving an elevated mental state through spiritual disciplines like prayer and meditation. This book is meant to point the reader to direct unmediated awareness of God. Complete, all-consuming, experiential oneness with God.

My life as a Christian pastor has convinced me that most religious people hunger for first-hand experience of the Divine. They are not very interested in religion with its doctrines, rituals, commandments and bureaucracies. They will not settle for church programs, self-help workshops or spiritual novelties. They do not need more spiritual books on their bookshelves or more spiritual insights in their minds. They may put up with organized religion and spiritual teachers, but only if they might lead to a genuine spiritual encounter.

Nondual Christianity is experiential spirituality. It is an immediate experience of oneness with God, Christ, and all of Creation. It is unity with all that exists. This may sound like pantheism to some Christians, but I assure you it is not. Pantheism is a religious philosophy, a philosophical worldview, an intellectual understanding of the universe. Christian nonduality is not an intellectual understanding. It is a direct apprehension of the Divine. It transcends thought and religion.

Divine Reality is by nature beyond the reach of human language. Some purists will say that to talk about "Christian nonduality" is already dualistic. Nondualism cannot be Christian, or any religion for that matter. Religions, including Christianity, are relative and part of this dualistic world. That is true.

But you have to describe nondualism somehow. If we are going to try to communicate the Unspeakable, we have to use language. Religious traditions have developed a culturally established vocabulary to describe spiritual experience. The vocabulary I know best is the language of Christianity. Therefore I describe nonduality in Christian terms.

Expressed in language more familiar to Christians, this book is about knowing God. It is about recognizing the Unity that we already have, the One "in whom we live and move and have our Being," as the apostle Paul described God to the Athenian philosophers. (Acts 17:28)

Nonduality is another word for oneness. Oneness makes positive statements about the underlying unity of all Existence. "Truth is this and this...." Nonduality comes at it from a different direction. It points to Truth by eliminating what it is not. It is "not this, not that." Nonduality is the "via negativa" of Christian spirituality. This is the way of Christian mystics. Both Oneness and Nonduality point to the same Truth. For that reason I use the two terms interchangeably.

The famous shema of the Hebrew tradition says, "Hear, O Israel: The Lord our God, the Lord is One. You shall love the Lord your God with all your heart, with all your soul, and with all your strength." (Deuteronomy 6:4-5) The Holy One of Israel is the Nondual Reality that Jews and Christians call God.

The New Testament teaches that everyone already knows God. The apostle John taught that Christ is the Divine Logos "that enlightens every man who comes into the world." (John 1:9) The apostle Paul taught, "What may be known of God is manifest in them [referring to those who do not acknowledge God], for God has shown it to them. For since the creation of the world His invisible attributes are clearly seen, being understood by the things that are made, even His eternal power and Godhead, so that they are without excuse" (Romans 1:19-20) Everyone already knows God. But people "suppress the truth in unrighteousness." (Romans 1:18) We refuse to consciously acknowledge what we intuitively know to be true. We have intentionally forgotten who God is and who we are.

Therefore you already know what this book is about. You just might not know that you know. I can't tell you anything in this book that you don't already know. I could not describe nonduality to you, even if I tried. Words are by nature dualistic. They operate by distinguishing "this" from "that." Nonduality is neither "this" nor "that." It is One.

Fortunately I don't need to describe nonduality, because you already know. You just need to remember (which literally means "to come back together.") My goal is to remind you of what you instinctively know is true, but will not admit.

Although words cannot describe Oneness, some words seem to have the ability to elicit memories of those times in our lives when we have been consciously aware of the Real. Although memories of nonduality are not the same thing as present awareness of nonduality, memories can help us recognize it now.

My memories of such times are accompanied by a wistful sense of recalling something long-forgotten. It is like déjà vu. It has a feeling of familiarity. It is recognition (re-knowing) of a truth that I did not even know I knew. That is why when we hear someone speak truth, we recognize it instantly, although we cannot explain how we know it is true. It resonates with something deep within us. In my life these experiences carry the scent of nostalgia, a longing for a forgotten home, a yearning to return and lose myself in its Edenic joy and peace.

In my life this awareness has often happened in natural settings of beauty and grandeur. Open spaces elicit openness in me. A mountain vista. An ocean seascape. A rocky stream. A mighty river. The Grand Canyon. The Milky Way. Sitting by a lake at dawn. As the psalmist says, "Deep calls to deep." (Psalm 42:7)

When I learned contemplative prayer, I discovered that this open spaciousness, which I experienced in Nature, was not in the external landscape but the inner one. I had not discovered peace in the wilderness; I had brought it into the wilderness. Openness goes with me, and I can see it anywhere. It is Home. Love. Joy. Peace. God.

C.S. Lewis describes an experience from his childhood. He calls it being "surprised by joy" in his book by the same name. He writes:

"The first is itself the memory of memory. As I stood beside a flowering currant bush on a summer day there suddenly arose in me without warning, as if from a depth not of years but of centuries, the memory of that earlier morning at the Old House when my brother had brought his toy garden into the nursery. It is difficult to find words strong enough for the sensation which came over me; Milton's 'enormous bliss' of Eden (giving the full, ancient meaning to enormous) comes somewhere near it. It was a sensation, of course, of desire; but of desire for what? Not, certainly, for a biscuit tin filled with moss, nor even (though that came into it) for my own past - and before I knew what I desired, the desire itself was gone, the whole glimpse withdrawn, the world turned commonplace again, or only stirred by a longing for the longing which had just ceased. It had taken only a moment of time; and in a certain sense everything else that had ever happened to me was insignificant in comparison." (Lewis, C.S., *Surprised By Joy*, pp. 22-23)

Such glimpses of nondual awareness are not uncommon. They are a common part of childhood. They are experienced by nearly everyone, although most people dismiss them as unimportant and quickly forget them. They do not realize that such experiences are an invitation from Eternity. This is a book about this direct awareness of Oneness.

Blaise Pascal knew this Oneness, as evidenced in his "Memorial," a scrap of paper found in the lining of his coat after his death. He carried this reminder of his experience with him always. It records Pascal's experience on one unforgettable night in 1654. The opening words of this intimate document reads:

Monday, 23 November, feast of St. Clement, pope and martyr, and others in the martyrology. Vigil of St. Chrysogonus, martyr, and others.

From about half past ten at night until about half past midnight,
FIRE.
GOD of Abraham, GOD of Isaac, GOD of Jacob
not of the philosophers and of the learned.
Certitude. Certitude. Feeling. Joy. Peace.
GOD of Jesus Christ.
My God and your God.
Your GOD will be my God.
Forgetfulness of the world and of everything, except GOD.

In Christian spirituality this experience of Oneness is usually called "union with God" or "communion with God." (Communion literally means "union with.") In her 1911 classic work "Mysticism: A Study of the Nature and Development of Man's Spiritual

Consciousness," the great Christian writer Evelyn Underhill called it the Unitive Life. I use a variety of terms, but most often Awareness, the Kingdom of God, or Presence.

This book is an exploration of this nondual Christian consciousness. It is written for Christians who have tasted this reality firsthand and don't know how to describe it using the pietistic language of American Christianity. They are looking for words to express their spiritual experience and a way to integrate their experience with Christian theology.

Christians who have had unitive experiences of the Divine often abandon their native Christian religious vocabulary and adopt Hindu or Buddhist terminology to describe their experience. This is unfortunate and unnecessary. There is a real need these days to express this spiritual awareness to Westerners using Christian concepts. The teachings of Jesus, as well as those of the apostles John and Paul, shine with the knowledge of the Oneness of God. Christian doctrines such as the Incarnation and the Trinity can be understood only from a nondual perspective.

I hope this book will also be read by those outside of Western spiritual traditions. I have found that Americans who have embraced Eastern religious spirituality often misunderstand Christianity. They tend to know only the neighborhood church variety or the parody of historic Christianity preached by fundamentalists. They tend to stereotype Christianity as dualistic, legalistic, and overly concerned with dogma. That is not the case. Christianity is nondualistic at its heart.

It is certainly true that the terms nonduality and Christianity are not usually found together. There are some exceptions. Father Richard Rohr of the Franciscan order spoke about the relationship between nonduality and Christianity at the Science and Nonduality Conference in 2011. He sees Christianity as essentially nondualistic, and points to the doctrine of Christ as an example. But according to him, nonduality never had a chance to flourish in the Christian West because of Christianity's early theological marriage to Greek dualistic philosophy.

Bede Griffiths, a British Benedictine monk, tried to combine Vedanta and his Christian faith, and formed ashrams in South India to that end. Thomas Merton explored it near the end of his life. Trappist monk Thomas Keating has communicated the experience of oneness with God through the teaching of Centering Prayer. More recently Francis Bennett, a former Trappist monk, has written about nonduality in his book "I Am That I Am." But this approach still remains rare in Christian circles.

When it does occur, it is usually voiced by those from the Roman Catholic monastic tradition, as evidenced by the examples just given. I am a Baptist. In fact I would acknowledge the term evangelical to describe my religious persuasion, although I seldom use this term because of its connotations in popular American culture.

I have been a Baptist minister serving as a pastor in mainline and evangelical congregations for 40 years, and my experience and understanding of Reality is nondualistic. How I came to this understanding is a story that might have value to some readers. For that reason I have included a brief account of my spiritual journey in the final chapter of this book. But my story is not really important. In fact it can be a distraction from the communication of the eternal reality of the oneness of God.

What is important to understand is that nonduality is not at odds with Christianity. This might come as a surprise to some Christians, especially those working in the area of Christian apologetics. For many conservative and evangelical Christians, "East is East and West is West and never the twain shall meet." Nondualism is equated with pantheism and considered to be opposed to the biblical theistic worldview. I know this mindset well because I was a proponent of this type of Christian apologetic for many years.

In reality Nondualism transcends all ideas, philosophies and religions. The Kingdom of God (which is Jesus' term for nondual Reality) is beyond theology. Theologies are only useful when they point beyond themselves to the Kingdom. That is why Jesus spoke in parables rather than give theological lectures. But more about that in the next chapter. Now I invite readers to recognize for themselves the Reality of which Jesus and the apostles spoke. It is nothing other than God, the One without a second. "I am the LORD, and there is no other besides me." Isaiah 45:5.

1

JESUS AS A PROCLAIMER OF NONDUALITY

"I and the Father are One."

- Jesus of Nazareth

Jesus was a proclaimer of the nondual Presence of God. He called it the Kingdom of God. According to the gospels, his earliest message was, "Repent, for the Kingdom of God is at hand." (Matthew 3:2; Mark 1:15) We would use different language today. The word "kingdom" is a concept from another time and place. Today most people have no personal experience with kings and kingdoms. A somewhat better translation for our day might be the Realm of

God. That would keep the royal imagery yet widens the concept.

An even better translation of Kingdom of God for today would be the Presence of God or the Omnipresence of God. "Omnipresence" is one of those theological terms that is not used in ordinary conversation. In fact it is seldom used outside of academic theological discourse. Yet it is one of the basic tenets of Christian theology. Omnipresence refers to the all-pervading presence of God. God is in all places at all times.

This is more than a theological doctrine. It is a living awareness available to everyone. Christian theology is practical and not theoretical. Theology is best understood as a description of our experience of God. To say that God is omnipresent is not just saying something about the nature of God. It says something about our experience of God. It describes my experience of God.

To experience this Presence, Jesus calls us to repent. That is another awkward term, which is often colored with moralistic overtones. The word "repent" literally means "to rethink." Jesus was saying, "Think again! God is here. Reach out and touch! See for yourself!"

Even the word God is misleading. It means different things to different people. The Muslim means one thing, a Hindu another, and a Native American still another. As I use the word, it refers to the one undefinable unnamable Divine Reality. "For my thoughts are not your thoughts, neither are your ways my ways," says the God of the Hebrew scriptures. (Isaiah 55:8)

God is omnipresent. Anyone with eyes to see can see God. God is everywhere. You can't miss God. As Jesus said, "Whoever has ears to hear, let them hear." I would add: Whoever has eyes to see, let them see.

Jesus' Awakening

Most Christians do not think about Jesus having a conversion experience. But the gospels clearly describe a moment when Jesus' life changed, and he woke up to his true nature and identity. As an adolescent, Jesus first got a glimpse of his true nature at his bar mitzvah at the age of twelve. The rabbis and religious leaders were amazed at his understanding as they conversed with him in the temple courts. He expressed an intimacy with God as his Father that was uncommon. But this was only an early glimpse of the fullness that was to come later.

At the age of thirty, Jesus had what one could call an awakening. On the day he was baptized he became fully aware of his identity as the Son of God. The Hebraic expression "son of" means "one who shares characteristics with" or "one who shares the nature of." James and John, two of Jesus' disciples, were known as the "sons of thunder" because of their fiery tempers. Joseph, a traveling companion of the apostle Paul, was given the name Barnabas, which means "son of encouragement."

Son of God means one who shares the nature and character of God. Adam is called the Son of God, (Luke 3:38) and his descendants were called Sons of God. (Genesis 6:2) But by Jesus' day, the expression Son of God was a claim to divinity. Caesar was called the Son of God. Consequently it was considered blasphemy by the religious establishment.

All four of the gospels record Jesus' baptism as a seminal event in his life. Jesus had listened to the preaching of the wilderness prophet John, whom many scholars theorize was associated with the ascetic Qumran community near the Dead Sea.

Jesus came to the Jordan River to be baptized by John. The gospels say that during this baptism, "the heavens were opened to him" (Matthew 3:16) and the Spirit of God descended upon him and remained on him. He heard the voice of God calling him his beloved Son. Jesus understood himself as one with God's Divine Nature.

This experience transformed Jesus' life. From that moment on he was the Christ, which means "the anointed one," anointed with the Spirit of God. This was a consciousness of God that was permanent. John described the change in Jesus' life by saying that the Spirit of God "remained on him" as opposed to the fleeting spiritual experiences of the Spirit, which were typical of other Hebrew prophets.

Jesus' awakening to his true nature and identity was followed by a time of integration. Jesus immediately retreated by himself into the wilderness. There in solitude he was "tempted by the devil." Three temptations challenged Jesus' new identity as the Son of God. In the end Jesus believed the voice of God rather than the voice of doubt. Jesus returned from the wilderness with a clear message, calling others to experience the Presence of God for themselves.

Pointing with Parables

Jesus had a unique style of teaching. He taught "as one having authority, not as the scribes," (Matthew 7:29) meaning that he spoke from his own self-authenticating experience of God. His teaching was not a secondhand reinterpretation of scripture and tradition. Often he would emphasize the discontinuity between his teachings and traditional religious teachings by saying, "You have heard that it was said of old, but I say unto you ....."

One distinctive teaching method that Jesus employed was the parable. Parables are metaphors, similes, or allegories meant to convey spiritual truth. Truth is a mystery that cannot be spoken of directly. It can only be referred to obliquely through the use of illustrations. These "pointers to truth" hide truth as well as reveal it. Only those who are spiritually ready to receive the message could hear it. Others would miss the point completely. The Gospel of Matthew records this interchange between Jesus and his disciples:

And the disciples came and said to Him, "Why do You speak to them in parables?" He answered and said to them, "Because it has been given to you to know the mysteries of the kingdom of heaven, but to them it has not been given. For whoever has, to him more will be given, and he will have abundance; but whoever does not have, even what he has will be taken away from him. Therefore I speak to them in parables, because seeing they do not see, and hearing they do not hear, nor do they understand. And in them the prophecy of Isaiah is fulfilled, which says:

'Hearing you will hear and shall not understand,
And seeing you will see and not perceive;
For the hearts of this people have grown dull.
Their ears are hard of hearing,
And their eyes they have closed,
Lest they should see with their eyes and hear
with their ears,
Lest they should understand with their hearts and
turn,
So that I should heal them.'

But blessed *are* your eyes for they see, and your ears for they hear." (Matthew 13:10-16)

The parables of Jesus are comparable to koans in the Zen tradition. The Japanese word "koan" means "a public teaching." Like parables koans were meant to be heard publicly. And like parables, only those ready to receive it would be transformed by it. All others would be deaf and blind to its spiritual intent.

Parables point beyond themselves to a spiritual reality that is not communicable in thoughts or ideas. They are meant to shift the consciousness of the hearer so that they can "see that which is invisible" as the Letter to the Hebrews describes it. (Hebrews 11:27)

Jesus' parables often speak of how the Kingdom of God is revealed. Jesus commonly used agricultural illustrations to describe the Kingdom as a natural process that grows unnoticed in the world and in the human heart until one day it blossoms into full realization.

Jesus said, "The kingdom of God is as if a man should scatter seed on the ground, and should sleep by night and rise by day, and the seed should sprout and grow, he himself does not know how. For the earth yields crops by itself: first the blade, then the head, after that the full grain in the head. But when the grain ripens, immediately he puts in the sickle, because the harvest has come." (Mark 4:26-29) The Kingdom is a mystery. It is does not appear by human effort, nor can it be understood by human knowledge. It is a natural process that one day blooms into fullness.

Jesus said, "To what shall we liken the kingdom of God? Or with what parable shall we picture it? It is like a mustard seed which, when it is sown on the ground, is smaller than all the seeds on earth; but when it is sown, it grows up and becomes greater than all herbs, and shoots out large branches, so that the birds of the air may nest under its shade." (Mark 4:30-32) The Kingdom of God can begin with a tiny insight or flash of intuition. But slowly it grows into full awareness of the Divine.

Sometimes the Kingdom dawns gradually like a seed growing in a field. At other times the Kingdom comes suddenly and unexpectedly. Jesus told several parables to that effect. Jesus spoke often about "the coming of the Son of Man." The phrase "Son of Man" was Jesus' favorite term to refer to himself. The "coming of the Son of Man" was another way of speaking about the coming of the Kingdom of God.

Jesus said, "For the Son of Man is coming at an hour you do not expect." (Luke 12:40) He said, "And they will say to you, 'Look here!' or 'Look there!' Do not go after them or follow them. For as the lightning that flashes out of one part under heaven shines to the other part under heaven, so also the Son of Man will be in His day." (Luke 17:23-24) The Kingdom of God can come upon a person like a lightning strike.

Often Christians understand the Kingdom of God in such "apocalyptic" passages as a cataclysmic event coming in the future, which is ushered in by the physical visible return of Jesus from heaven. But the Kingdom of God does not have to be understood as an historical event happening in the distant future.

Jesus said, "Assuredly, I say to you that there are some standing here who will not taste death till they see the Kingdom of God present with power." (Matthew 16:28)

This verse has caused great consternation to Christians who understand the Kingdom of God exclusively as a future event occurring in history. Such a kingdom did not come in the lifetimes of the people who heard Jesus speak these words. This is a serious problem for literalists. It means that either Jesus made a mistake or that he was a false prophet, both of which are unacceptable alternatives for Christians. To find a suitable solution, interpreters have performed hermeneutical gymnastics to twist Jesus' words to fit a preconception of the Kingdom as an eschatological event in the future.

But when the verse is understood as referring to a person who sees the invisible Presence of God, the saying makes perfect sense. Jesus is simply saying that some of the people who were listening to his words would personally "see the Kingdom of God present with power." These persons would become aware of God's Presence during their lifetimes.

On another occasion Jesus was performing exorcisms, and he said, "If I cast out demons by the Spirit of God, surely the kingdom of God has come upon you." (Luke 11:20) Clearly Jesus taught that the Kingdom of God was already present, as evidenced in his ministry.

Jesus also said, "The kingdom of God does not come with observation; nor will they say, 'See here!' or 'See there!' For indeed, the kingdom of God is within you." (Luke 17:20-21) An alternate translation of the verse reads: "the Kingdom of God is in your midst." Both translations are acceptable. The Kingdom of God is both within and without. In the Gospel of Thomas Jesus says, "The kingdom of the Father is spread out upon the earth, and men do not see it." (Thomas 113) The Kingdom of God is present here now but only those with eyes to see can see it.

Christians do not have to choose between these two interpretations of the Kingdom of God as present Reality or prophetic future event. For those who view the Kingdom of God as an eschatological event in the future, there are enough biblical texts to support that claim. For those who adhere to a "realized eschatology" of the Kingdom as a present Reality, there are numerous texts to support that view. Jesus taught both views. In a parallel manner, nonduality teachers today speak about a conscious awareness of Oneness now and also about a future time when the whole earth will experience an evolutionary shift in consciousness.

Christians who see the Kingdom of God now know it as eternal and timeless. Those who do not see the present Kingdom now await a Kingdom coming in the future. Both are true. There need be no contradiction between the two. Truth is nondual. The two realities are one. When the kingdom comes in history it will be here now, as it always has been. The only time it can ever appear is in the present.

2

UNBORN AGAIN

"Most assuredly, I say to you, unless one is born again, he cannot see the kingdom of God."

– Jesus of Nazareth

Evangelical Christians are not born again. That is my assessment from ministering among evangelicals for most of my life. I know evangelicals well. I would consider myself one. I earned two graduate degrees from the Southern Baptist Theological Seminary in Louisville, Kentucky. I have served as senior pastor of Southern Baptist churches and American Baptist churches (a more moderate, but still evangelical denomination.) I have known evangelicals – clergy and laity – for a long time. My opinion is that very few are "born again" in the way that Jesus describes it.

I am not suggesting that evangelicals are not "saved," in the way in which they understand salvation – in terms of life in heaven after death. Evangelicals certainly believe in Jesus Christ as Lord and Savior, and they trust in Christ for eternal life. If that is what it means to be born again, then evangelicals are born again. That is what evangelicals mean by the term "born again," but that is not what Jesus meant when he used that phrase.

Let's listen to what Jesus actually said. The story is found in John's Gospel. Jesus is having a conversation with Nicodemus, a member of the Sanhedrin, the Jewish religion's ruling council. Nicodemus had previously heard Jesus teach, and he was interested enough in his message to want to hear more. Because of the controversial nature of Jesus' ministry, and to protect his own reputation as a religious leader, Nicodemus decided to make a clandestine visit to the Galilean preacher. He came to see Jesus under the cover of darkness. Here is the exchange between the two men as recorded in the Gospel of John:

> There was a man of the Pharisees named Nicodemus, a ruler of the Jews. This man came to Jesus by night and said to Him, "Rabbi, we know that You are a teacher come from God; for no one can do these signs that You do unless God is with him."

Jesus answered and said to him, "Most assuredly, I say to you, unless one is born again, he cannot see the kingdom of God."

Nicodemus said to Him, "How can a man be born when he is old? Can he enter a second time into his mother's womb and be born?"

Jesus answered, "Most assuredly, I say to you, unless one is born of water and the Spirit, he cannot enter the kingdom of God. That which is born of the flesh is flesh, and that which is born of the Spirit is spirit. Do not marvel that I said to you, 'You must be born again.' The wind blows where it wishes, and you hear the sound of it, but cannot tell where it comes from and where it goes. So is everyone who is born of the Spirit."

Nicodemus answered and said to Him, "How can these things be?"

Jesus answered and said to him, "Are you the teacher of Israel, and do not know these things? Most assuredly, I say to you, We speak what We know and testify what We have seen, and you do not receive Our witness. If I have told you earthly things and you do not believe, how will you believe if I tell you heavenly things?"

That is the end of the conversation between the two men. After this exchange the Gospel writer (traditionally considered to be the apostle John) speaks about the importance of believing in Christ and having eternal life through faith in Jesus. The passage culminates in the most beloved of all evangelical verses, John 3:16: "For God so loved the world that He gave His only begotten Son, that whoever believes in Him should not perish but have everlasting life."

Belief in Christ is central to the Christian faith of the early church. But it was not what Jesus was talking about when he told Nicodemus that he had to be born again. According to Jesus, being born again means to see the Kingdom of God. Jesus said, "Most assuredly, I say to you, unless one is born again, he cannot see the kingdom of God." The traditional language says "Verily, verily, I say to you...." Jesus uses this preamble whenever he wants to emphasize what follows. Jesus is saying that if one is born again he will absolutely, positively, see the Kingdom of God.

Would any evangelical say they see the Kingdom of God? Not too many that I know! They would say that they are looking forward to seeing the Kingdom of God when Jesus returns in glory. They would say that they expect to enter into the Kingdom of Heaven when they die. They might go so far as to say that they believe they have in a spiritual sense entered the Kingdom of God now, insofar as they believe they have been saved. But very few would say that they see the Kingdom of God or that they have entered the Kingdom of God in its fullness. Yet that is exactly what Jesus says it means to be "born of the Spirit" or "born again."

Being "born again" is a direct experience of the Presence of God here now. When one is born of the Spirit, one immediately enters the Kingdom of God and sees the Kingdom of God. A door opens before one's eyes and one's view of the universe is transformed.

Nicodemus hears Jesus' teaching about being born again, but he immediately resists it. It was too radical – too much, too soon. He expected a little small talk first before they got into the heavy stuff. He expected a little theological repartee between colleagues. But instead Jesus immediately lays it all out before him: "Most assuredly, I say to you, unless one is born again, he cannot see the kingdom of God."

Jesus' words struck a chord in Nicodemus' heart, and he was afraid. He could feel the ground shifting beneath his feet. In an instinctive reaction of self-defense, Nicodemus comes back with a seemingly silly statement about returning into his mother's womb to be born a second time. "How can a man be born when he is old? Can he enter a second time into his mother's womb and be born?"

In actuality, he was utilizing a classic rhetorical device. In Latin it is called "reductio ad absurdum." It was well known in Greek debating, and also well known among the Jewish rabbis of the first century.

"Reductio ad absurdum" demonstrates that a statement is false by showing the absurdity that follows from its acceptance. "How can a man go back into his mother's womb and be born again? Ridiculous!"

Jesus will not be sidetracked by Nicodemus' debating skills. He rewords it and says that one must be "born of the Spirit." Then Jesus explains this spiritual transformation using other words. "That which is born of the flesh is flesh, and that which is born of the Spirit is spirit. Do not marvel that I said to you, 'You must be born again.' The wind blows where it wishes, and you hear the sound of it, but cannot tell where it comes from and where it goes. So is everyone who is born of the Spirit."

Jesus is saying that being born again is a spiritual reality, not a physical one. He describes it as like the wind blowing through the Palestinian countryside. "The wind blows where it wishes, and you hear the sound of it, but cannot tell where it comes from and where it goes. So is everyone who is born of the Spirit." Jesus describes being spiritually reborn in terms of unknowing. We don't know where the wind comes from and where it is going. (It is helpful to know that the Greek and Hebrew words for wind can also be translated spirit.) One who is born again doesn't know if he is coming or going. He is just blowing in the wind.

This is a description of nondual awareness. Nonduality is best described in terms of what it is not. In classic Christian spirituality this is known as the via negativa, the way of negation. It is also known as negative theology or apophatic theology (from the Greek word meaning "to deny"). Being born again is "not this" and "not that." If you try to describe it, you are missing it. Nothing one can say about it is true without immediately saying the opposite. Even balancing a statement with its opposite misses the mark, because it makes the truth dualistic, and God is nondual. The Lord is One.

Jesus was pointing Nicodemus beyond the common theistic experience of first century Judaism to a direct awareness of the Nondual God. Jesus gave a similar teaching on other occasions when he said that one has to become like a little child to enter the Kingdom of God. That means the same as being "born again." A little child has not yet developed the psychological sense of a personal self that separates him from the rest of the world. He is still one. The little child does not experience himself as other than God or God's creation. On the Sermon on the Mount Jesus taught, "Blessed are the pure in heart, for they shall see God." Little children are pure in heart. To see God one must become a little child again. One must be born again.

I AM

Jesus said, "Before Abraham was, I AM." Jesus was saying that before Abraham was born, and before he himself was born, that his true nature is Eternal. Jesus' true nature is unborn. Centuries later in the Nicene Creed, Christian theologians would describe Jesus' nature as "eternally begotten of the Father, God from God, Light from Light, true God from true God, begotten, not made, one in Being with the Father." Jesus' self-understanding was heretical in that time and place. The gospel story says that the religious leaders who heard Jesus speak these words picked up stones with the intent to execute him by stoning. These radical words are the essence of Jesus' consciousness, and they are the essence of the Christian's identity in Christ.

In using the words "I AM," Jesus was making reference to a story about Moses recorded in the Book of Exodus. It was Moses' awakening experience. To use traditional Christian terminology, it was his conversion. It happened when Moses was a happily married family man living in the mountains of Midian in the Sinai Peninsula. Moses had been raised in the religious traditions of Egypt as the grandson of the Pharaoh. But after committing murder, he fled Egypt and settled in Midian. There he married into a local tribe and embraced the Semitic theism of his wife and father-in-law.

One day while tending the family flock in the wilderness, Moses had a dramatic spiritual encounter. Its visual manifestation was a burning bush, an eternal flame that did not consume its earthly fuel. From the bush the One God spoke to Moses. God told Moses to free the Hebrews from bondage. Hebrew religious tradition understood this as freedom from the physical bondage of slavery in Egypt, but a fuller understanding would be liberation from spiritual bondage.

When Moses asked this One's name, God refused. He is the Unnamable. But at the insistence of Moses, God relented. For practical reasons Moses needed some Name to give his people. God replied, "I am who I am. Tell them I AM sent you." (Exodus 3:14)

When Jesus identified himself as I AM, he was equating himself with the Eternal God. Throughout the Gospel of John Jesus makes repeated reference to himself as I AM. "I AM the Light of the World. I AM the Bread of Life. I AM the Way, the Truth and the Life." The self-identity "I AM" is the unifying theme of this gospel.

In his prologue, John makes it clear who he understands Christ to be. "In the beginning was the Word, and the Word was with God and the Word was God.... And the Word became flesh and dwelt among us and we beheld his glory, the glory of the only begotten of the Father, full of grace and truth.... No one has seen God at any time. The only begotten

God, who is in the bosom of the Father, He has declared Him." (John 1:1, 14, 18)

Not only is this divine consciousness the experience of Jesus, it is also the experience of Jesus' followers. In the prayer of Jesus, which was offered shortly before his arrest and death, Jesus makes it clear that he expects his followers to know this same Oneness.

Jesus prayed for his followers, "that they all may be one, as You, Father, are in Me, and I in You; that they also may be one in Us, that the world may believe that You sent Me. And the glory which You gave Me I have given them, that they may be one just as We are one: I in them, and You in Me; that they may be made perfect in one, and that the world may know that You have sent Me, and have loved them as You have loved Me." (John 17:21-23)

The followers of Christ share the Oneness that Jesus had. The awareness of Oneness was supposed to be the distinguishing characteristic of Christians, and the means that would draw people to faith in Christ. Jesus was a proclaimer of nonduality, and he prayed that his followers would experience the same Oneness that he knew.

3

SELF-INQUIRY

"It is not I who live, but Christ who lives in me."
- Apostle Paul

"Know thyself" was the Greek inscription that greeted ancient pilgrims at the entrance to the temple at Delphi. This admonition is the most basic expression of the spiritual search. Even before one can seek God, one must know who it is who seeks God. When one knows oneself, everything else becomes clearer. Discovery of our true nature opens our eyes to the true nature of God and the world.

The psalmist mused, "What is man that thou art mindful of him?" (Psalm 8:4) Historically, the answer given to that question by Christianity has been that humans are physical beings made by a Creator. We are creatures composed of a mortal body and an immortal soul. That dualism is what most Christians believe. But that is not what the Christian scriptures teach. This body-soul division came from Greek philosophy, which was baptized into Christianity very early in the history of the Church.

The Hebrew and Christian Scriptures teach that man is one. Like God, humans are understood as trinity: three in one. The apostle Paul wrote, "Now may the God of peace Himself sanctify you wholly; and may your whole spirit, soul, and body be preserved blameless...." (I Thessalonians 5:23) In New Testament Christianity, a human being is an integrated whole, composed of physical body, personal soul, and eternal spirit.

The creation story in the book of Genesis describes the tripartite origin of man. "And the Lord God formed man of the dust of the ground, and breathed into his nostrils the breath of life; and man became a living soul." (Genesis 2:7) Humans have bodies formed from the elements of the earth. The Hebrew word for man is the masculine form of the word for earth. Etymologically speaking, humans are literally "earthlings." We are made from earth, and those earthly elements return to earth at our physical death – earth to earth, ashes to ashes, dust to dust. Ecclesiastes says, "The dust will return to the earth as it was, and the spirit will return to God who gave it." (Ecclesiastes 12:7)

The body is temporary. It is 'born and it dies. Between those temporal end points, the body is continually changing. Every part of our bodies is constantly being born and dying. Every cell of our body is replaced every seven years. Physically speaking, we are not the same person we were seven years ago, much less seventy years ago. By the time we reach our seventieth year, we have been physically "reincarnated" ten times. This simple insight into our physical nature reveals that our bodies are not our true nature. Yet we know intuitively that something about us has remained the same throughout the various versions of our physical bodies.

The second aspect of the human being is the soul. The conventional idea of the human soul is that it is a spiritual entity inhabiting a physical body and thought to survive the dissolution of the body. This concept of an immortal soul within a mortal body was imported into Christian thought from Plato and Aristotle. Plato taught that the soul lived in the body "like an oyster in a shell." Although this is now the common understanding of the soul, it is not the Biblical view.

In Biblical thought, a human being does not have a soul; a human being IS a soul. In the Genesis account of creation, God breathed "the breath of life" into the physical body of man, and he "became a living soul." God's spirit-breath [the Hebrew word can be translated spirit, breath, or wind] acted as a catalyst, interacting with earthly elements to form an entirely new entity called the soul. There is no preexistent or immortal soul in Hebraic or Christian thought. The soul begins at birth.

The Greek word for soul is psyche. The soul is best understood as the psychological self. The popularizer of this Biblical understanding was the 20th century Chinese theologian Watchman Nee, an evangelical Christian leader who died in prison at the hands of the communists. In his three-volume work "The Spiritual Man," Nee demonstrates that the Scriptures teach that the soul has three faculties – intellect, emotion, and volition. These can also be described as mind, heart, and will.

The soul is the human personality, sometimes called the ego. It is our sense of being a personal entity. It is our persona. It is what it means to be a person. It is gradually formed during the early years of childhood and dominates our adult lives. We are born with genetic attributes that interact with our environment and develop into a unique self-conscious individual. A child forms a sense of a separate self during the first three years of life. From that time on, we identify ourselves with our psyche. This self is given a name and plays roles in family and society. The self is influenced by life experiences and comes to understand itself as having a personal history. For all practical purposes we come to believe that we ARE our self or soul. Nearly everyone identifies themselves by the distinctive manifestations of their self – their thoughts, feelings, desires, and choices.

But upon close inspection it can be seen that this personal self is no more permanent than the body. In fact it is even less substantial than the body. The self is nothing more than a mental fabrication of the brain, which in turn is simply an organ of the body. Therefore the self dies when the brain dies with the body. If we are looking for our essential nature, then it is clear that we are not our soul – our individual, personal, psychological self – any more than we are our bodies.

The third aspect of human being is spirit. In Genesis the spirit was breathed into the human body to produce the human soul. At death the body returns to the earth, the soul ceases to exist (since it has no real existence apart from the body) and the spirit returns to Spirit. The author of Ecclesiastes says, "The dust will return to the earth as it was, and the spirit will return to God who gave it." (Ecclesiastes 12:7) The spirit is what gives us life. We stay alive "as long as my breath is in me, and the breath of God in my nostrils." (Job 27:3) When it is withdrawn, we die.

What makes us conscious living beings is spirit. Human beings are spirit at the core. If we are looking for the part of human nature that is permanent - which survives death - then the only viable candidate is spirit. The spirit is not born and does not die. It has no beginning and no end. It comes from God and returns to God. In Genesis, the human spirit is "the breath of God." It is what makes us alive. It is the mystery that we call Life. This is who we are. We are life. And the gospel says of the Eternal Christ, "In Him was life, and the life was the light of men." (John 1:4)

Another way of communicating the same truth is to say that we are made in the image of God. This, in turn, is another way of saying that we are children of God. The apostle Paul says to the Athenian philosophers, "We are His offspring." (Acts 17:28) He says to the Roman Christians, "The Spirit Himself bears witness with our spirit that we are children of God." (Romans 8:14) These ideas are all metaphors to describe that dimension of our being that is one with God.

What is man? Most people perceive themselves to be individual selves with physical bodies. In actuality we are spirit, temporarily expressed as psychological physical beings. As Christian philosopher Pierre Teilhard de Chardin says, "We are not human beings having a spiritual experience; we are spiritual beings having a human experience."

What is spirit? Physically speaking it is nothing. It is literally "no thing." Spirit has no physical characteristics. Spirit is by definition nonmaterial. It is not matter. Neither is it energy. Matter and energy are different physical manifestations of the same thing. Matter turns into energy and energy into matter, in an ever-changing dance of duality. If spirit were energy, it could be empirically proven to exist by the scientific method. But it can't. Therefore it does not exist in the normal way of understanding existence. It is not part of this dualistic universe. Spirit is the word given to that which does not empirically exist, and yet is the foundation of all existence. It is Being from which all beings draw their existence.

Being beyond the duality of time and space, spirit is eternal. It is the only part of the human being that is eternally real. The Spirit of God formed everything else ex nihilo – out of nothing. God is the "No-thing" from which everything comes. God is the Nondual Reality that was before the birth of this dualistic universe in the Big Bang. God is that in which all things exist. As Paul says of God, "In Him we live and move and have our being." (Acts 17:28) If the spiritual search is the quest for what is Real, and if Reality is defined as that which does not change, then the only part of the human being that is real is spirit. Spirit is our true nature.

The Cross of Christ as the Door to the Real

The spiritual quest is to realize through direct experience who we really are and who God really is. As a child (before what Christians would call "the Fall") we knew this, but we did not know that we knew. We were conscious, but not self-conscious – aware but not self-aware. In childhood humans become lost in the tangle of the psyche. That is the real meaning of original sin. Every human being has eaten the fruit of duality, "the Tree of the Knowledge of Good and Evil." Humans have separated themselves from God and from their own true nature. We have believed our own thoughts. Soul reigns in place of Spirit.

Humans have mistaken their psyches for their real self, and consequently remade God in their own image. Man's self pictures God as a supreme Personal Self. Man's mind imagines God as Divine Intellect. God is seen as Super Man. As Rousseau said, "God created man in his own image. And man, being a gentleman, returned the favor." God made man as spirit in his own image as Spirit. But man has mistaken himself to be psyche and reimagined God as a Super Psyche. That religious image of God as a Big Self is no more real than the human psyche it was patterned after. It is nothing more than an idol. Consequently most theistic worship is little more than idolatry, the worship of man's own persona projected upon the fabric of the universe.

Spiritual inquiry is the search to discover our real self and the Real God. The Christian gospel says that this discovery of true self and True God is made through Jesus Christ. He is the door into what Christians call salvation, redemption or freedom. Jesus said, "If the Son makes you free, you shall be free indeed." (John 8:36) Jesus said, "I am the door; if anyone enters through Me, he will be saved." (John 10:9) To use Christian terminology, Christ is the mediator between God and man. In Christ is the union of spirit with Spirit - human spirit with Divine Spirit.

In Christian theology that reconciliation of man and God is understood as accomplished through the crucifixion and resurrection of Jesus Christ. Christian theology has devoted much time to explaining exactly how the execution of a first century preacher accomplished eternal salvation. Most of it is based on the dualistic understanding of man, God, and the world.

From a nondual perspective, the Cross takes on a whole new meaning. The Cross is seen as the destruction of the body and soul (self) of Jesus and the survival of the Spirit of Jesus. As the apostle Paul writes, "The first man Adam became a living being. The last Adam [referring to Jesus] became a life-giving spirit." (I Corinthians 15:45) In the crucifixion, the physical body of Jesus died. The Gospel writers emphasize the fact that Jesus really died. He did not fall unconscious only to be resuscitated later. Jesus did not have a Near Death experience; he had a Real Death experience. The New Testament and historic Christianity affirm the real physical death of Jesus.

The Cross is also the death of the self - or soul - of Jesus. The psychological suffering of Jesus' crucifixion is emphasized in the Gospels as much as his physical pain. Jesus cried out from the cross, "My God, my God, why hast Thou forsaken me?" (Matthew 27:46)

Many Christians struggle with this cry of anguish coming from the lips of their Savior. It seems inconsistent with a life of perfect faith in God. It is assumed that the Son of God should have slipped into Heaven in equanimity, like the Buddha sliding calmly into Nirvana at his death.

But from a nondual point of view, Jesus' cry of agony makes perfect sense. It is the death cry of the personal self, which perceives itself headed for extinction. The crucifixion of Jesus depicts the death of the self, which did not "go gentle into that good night." This death of the self of Jesus is as important as the death of the body of Jesus. Once the crucifixion had accomplished its purpose of extinguishing the self, the only thing left for Jesus to do was to surrender his spirit to God. Finally Jesus said, "Father, into your hands I commit my spirit." Then he breathed his last. (Luke 23:46)

The Cross of Jesus is truly the way of salvation, the way of liberation from this earthly life to eternal life. The way of salvation is the death of the self and the release of the spirit. Jesus taught this repeatedly during his ministry for those who had the ears to hear. Jesus said, "If anyone would come after me, let him deny himself [his self] and take up his cross and follow me. For whoever seeks to save his life [the Greek word used is psyche] will lose it, and whoever loses his life will preserve it." (Matthew 16:24-25) Elsewhere he said, "And whoever does not bear his

cross and come after Me cannot be My disciple."
(Luke 14:27)

We die to self in order to live to God. Paul says, "I
have been crucified with Christ. It is no longer I who
live, but Christ who lives in me." (Galatians 2:20) He
says, "And those who belong to Christ Jesus have
crucified the sinful nature [Paul's term for self] with
its passions and desires." (Galatians 5:24 NIV) The
Cross of Christ depicts the physical death of the body
and the psychological death of the self. It reveals that
these parts of human nature are only temporary and,
in an ultimate sense, unreal.

The resurrection of Jesus is the second half of the
salvation story in the Gospels. The resurrection
illustrates the point that liberation is not a
disembodied state. It is not something that is
attainable only after the physical death of the body. It
is possible to live a spiritual life and still be in the
body. Therefore the Gospels emphasize the physical
nature of the resurrection of Jesus. It was the physical
body of Jesus along with the psychological self of
Jesus that was resurrected on the third day. The death
and resurrection of Jesus is not just a myth
communicating a truth about a "spiritual"
resurrection. The physical nature of the resurrection
stresses the fact that one can live a resurrected,
spiritually reborn life before physical death, while still
having a personal identity as a personal self. Christian
salvation is an incarnated spiritual life.

The Role of Faith

Faith in God and Christ are the hallmarks of Christianity. Indeed Christianity is often called the Christian faith. What is the role of faith in nondual Christianity? In historic Christianity, faith is chiefly a function of the self, involving one's intellect, emotion and volition. Faith believes certain intellectual assertions about God, Christ, and Spirit. This is the doctrinal part of Christianity. Faith involves a personal relationship with a Personal God. Evangelical Christians speak of having an intimate personal relationship with Jesus Christ. This is the devotional dimension of faith. Faith is making a personal decision to commit one's life to Christ as Lord and Savior. In these ways the term "faith" is a function of the personal self, what the Christian scriptures call the soul.

All these dimensions of faith are true. But faith is more than a soulical (to use Watchman Nee's term) activity. In a profounder way, faith is a dimension of nondual awareness. Faith trusts those first glimpses of Oneness. Faith trusts Christ and others who describe the reality of this Oneness. Faith dies to self in order to live to God. Faith trusts that the death of the self is not the end. It trusts that what appears to be death is actually life. Faith trusts glimpses of Oneness with God and is willing to love God with all one's heart, mind, soul and strength.

The vast majority of people ignore Oneness. They dismiss it as nothing (which is ironically exactly what it is!) Faith pays attention to this consciousness, even when its appearance is as tiny as a mustard seed. When attention is paid to Oneness, one's awareness of it grows. Faith trusts that this seemingly insignificant mode of perception is real. Faith believes it is true, even though the mind wants to dismiss it. Faith sees beyond the mind (the literal meaning of the Greek word for repentance "metanoia.") Faith surrenders to the Unknown and Unknowable, which is Spirit.

When one awakens to the Oneness of God, the world is seen from a different perspective. This is spiritual sight. It is seeing by faith. As the Letter of Hebrew famously puts it, "Now faith is the substance of things hoped for, the evidence of things not seen." (Hebrews 11:1) It is "seeing that which is invisible." (Hebrews 11:27) One sees with spirit, rather than with body or soul. As the apostle Paul says, "So from now on we regard no one from a worldly point of view. Though we once regarded Christ in this way, we do so no longer. Therefore, if anyone is in Christ, the new creation has come: The old has gone, the new is here!" (2 Corinthians 5:16-17 NIV) One comprehends the world from the perspective of spirit through the faculties of the spirit. Faith is the human spirit's faculty of apprehending nondual Reality. One sees by faith what cannot be seen with the eyes or understood with the mind. Faith sees directly and immediately. By faith one knows the true nature of Reality.

Like the soul, the human spirit also has three faculties, according to Watchman Nee's spiritual anthropology. The faculties of the spirit are intuition, conscience and communion. Faith is operable within each of these faculties. One sees the Kingdom of God through intuition. One knows Oneness intuitively. One acts instinctively by conscience without referring to an external Law of right and wrong. One lives in the Spirit and walks in the Spirit. "If you are led by the Spirit, you are not under the law." (Galatians 5:18)

Most importantly one has communion with the One God. The word communion means "union with." When Christians use this word they are usually referring to a feeling of closeness with the Personal God. This personal communion is real for the human soul, but there is a higher – or deeper – communion. What is true of the spirit does not negate what is true of the soul; it transcends it. Nondual awareness does not negate dualistic awareness. It includes it and fulfills it. In the same way Jesus said he did not come to abolish the Law but to fulfill it. (Matthew 5:17) The soul knows intimate fellowship with a Personal God by the devotional path. The spirit knows union with the Spirit by the contemplative path. Holy Spirit is one with human spirit.

By faith the Christian dies with Christ, is resurrected with Christ, and spiritually ascends to heaven with Christ to be united with God. That is what Brother Lawrence meant when he said, "I am assured beyond all doubt that my soul has been with GOD above these thirty years." The gospel story of the death, resurrection and ascension of Christ is not just a record of events that happened two thousand years ago to an individual named Jesus of Nazareth. It is also the way of the Christian's liberation from mortality and the bondage of the self, what the apostle Paul calls "the old man."

We are crucified with Christ and raised with Christ. Baptism symbolizes that transformation. "We were buried with Him through baptism into death, that just as Christ was raised from the dead by the glory of the Father, even so we also should walk in newness of life." (Romans 6:4) By faith we are one with Christ, having the mind of Christ (I Corinthians 2:16), and sharing the eternal life of Christ.

4

GOD INQUIRY

"I have heard of You by the hearing of the ear, but now my eye sees You." – Job

Thank God for atheists! They have revealed God to me! Atheists have taught me more about God than any preacher or seminary professor. They have shown me what God is not, and thereby pointed me toward who God is. I credit the books of the so-called "New Atheists" - people like Richard Dawkins, Daniel Dennett, Sam Harris, Victor Stenger, and Christopher Hitchens - with helping me identify and reject false gods and thereby redirect me to True God. Especially former Christian preachers who became atheists – people like John Loftus, Charles Templeton, and Dan Barker – have deepened my Christian faith by pointing out the weaknesses of traditional understandings of God.

These atheists are effective spiritual teachers because they are sincere inquirers into truth. They have investigated religious claims with uncompromising and relentless honesty. At the end of their inquiries, they have concluded that the God depicted by theistic religions does not exist. I agree with them... for the most part. In fact I am a card-carrying member of the Skeptics Society founded by atheist Michael Shermer. (I would not be surprised if I were the only active Christian pastor on their rolls!) I read Skeptic magazine religiously and agree with most of what it says. I do not believe in the God that atheists don't believe in. Atheist Richard Dawkins wrote, "We are all atheists about most of the gods that humanity has ever believed in. Some of us just go one god further." I go one step further than atheists. I reject the atheist concept of God as much as the conventional theistic concept of God.

But that does not make me an atheist. My inquiry into God – like my inquiry into the nature of the self – has led me beyond the human conceptions of God to what Christian philosopher Paul Tillich calls "God beyond God." The God of religion is nothing more than an idea in the mind. The God of most Christians is no more real than Santa Claus or the Tooth Fairy, albeit usually more philosophically sophisticated. (Usually, but not always!) The theistic God worshipped in most churches is no more than an imaginary Friend, a deity made in man's own image. It is a construction of the human mind, a mental image. To worship a mental image of God is just as idolatrous as worshiping a graven image, and it is just as much a violation of the first and second commandments.

The God of most theists is an idol. But God is real. The One God that Christian doctrines, icons, scriptures, and words point to is Ultimately Real. But ideas about God are not. We must not mistake the words used to describe God for God to whom they point. There is an old saying: Do not mistake the finger pointing to the moon for the moon itself. We must not mistake doctrine that points to Truth for Truth Itself. Road signs along the spiritual path are not the destination to which they point.

True God is without qualities and characteristics. God is without name. That is the point of the conversation that Moses had with God at the burning bush. God refused to give Moses His name because God is Nameless. Even today, Jews will not pronounce the theonym YHWH, the revealed Name of God. It is unpronounceable because it is unknowable. As the Tao Te Ching says, "The Tao that can be spoken of is not the Eternal Tao. The Name that can be named is not the Eternal Name." Tao is the Chinese word for what Christians call God or Christ. When Christians first translated the Gospel of John into Chinese they rendered the opening words: "In the Beginning was the Tao, and the Tao was with God, and the Tao was God." This remains the most widely used Chinese translation of the New Testament today.

There are two basic approaches to Divine Truth. One is self-inquiry, relentlessly pursuing the question, "Who am I?" until the answer is experienced directly and immediately. When we see who we truly are, we see who God truly is. The other way is to ask "Who is God?" When we know God, then we know ourselves. The first approach is most commonly used in Eastern spiritual traditions. The second approach is found in Western traditions. An equivalent question asked by Christians is "Who is Christ?" There are two ways of understanding Christ: Christology from below (beginning with Jesus' human nature) and Christology from above (starting with his divine nature.) When it comes to spiritual inquiry, East starts "from below," asking "Who am I?" West starts "from above," asking "Who is God?"

When Christians ask the question "Who is God?" it is usually answered with the doctrinal statements found in creeds and catechisms. But those are secondhand knowledge of God. In the Old Testament, Job had a lot of secondhand knowledge about God. He was a very religious and moral man. So were his friends, who came to comfort him when he lost everything in a series of catastrophes. But Job's theology did not help him when he was faced with intense personal suffering. He needed more than religious answers. He wanted direct knowledge of God. So he made an intense personal inquiry.

His search fills 36 chapters of the Book of Job. Job asked question after question, and eventually he found the answer. As Jesus would later promise, "Ask it and shall be given to you. Seek and you shall find." (Matthew 7:7) A traumatic series of losses - the death of his family, the loss of his possessions, the destruction of his reputation, and alienation from his wife and friends - ripped away all Job's previous beliefs about God. So he battered on heaven's door until God answered. At the end of the Book of Job God finally appeared in a whirlwind, and asks Job a series of questions:

"Who is this who darkens counsel
By words without knowledge?
Now prepare yourself like a man;
I will question you, and you shall answer Me.
"Where were you when I laid the foundations of the earth?
Tell Me, if you have understanding.
Who determined its measurements?
Surely you know!
Or who stretched the line upon it?
To what were its foundations fastened?
Or who laid its cornerstone,
When the morning stars sang together,
And all the sons of God shouted for joy? (Job 38:2-7)

These questions are the beginning of four chapters of unanswered and unanswerable questions posed by God. The purpose of these questions was to demonstrate to Job the impossibility of ever understanding God. They are designed to push Job beyond theology and theodicy into direct awareness of God. Finally Job gets it. His eyes are opened. He responds, "I have heard of You by the hearing of the ear, But now my eye sees You." (Job 42:5) Job received no theological or philosophical answers to his questions and doubts. He received far better. He saw God.

Paradoxical Pointers

In nondual Christianity, theology is not understood as a metaphysical description of Reality. It is a description of the Christian experience of the nondual nature of God. Theology describes human experience, not God. Doctrines are meant to push the Christian beyond thought to direct experience of God. Conventional Christianity has been known for its propositional theology, carefully distinguishing orthodoxy from heresy. But some central doctrines of Christianity do not fit that straitjacket. They are clearly meant to point beyond ideas. The two most important of these doctrines are the Trinity and the Incarnation.

The Christian doctrine of the Trinity describes God as Three in One - one monotheistic Deity in three divine Persons: Father, Son, and Holy Spirit. It attempts to combine Jewish monotheism with the Christian experience of God. God is experienced as both One and Three. In explaining the Trinity, theologians make it clear that God is not a Heavenly Triumvirate of deities. That would be polytheism, which is the boogeyman of the Hebrew and Christian scriptures. The Church also rejected any explanation that explained the Trinity as one God using three masks or having three functions. Christian theology insisted that God is truly One, and yet also Three.

Of course this is a logical impossibility, like the equation 1+1+1=1. That is not mathematically true. Neither is the Trinity "true" on the level of logic. The Trinity is meant to push the Christian believer beyond reason into a direct awareness of Mystery. God is not known with the mind. God is the Unknown, and can be apprehended only by unknowing. Like a Zen koan, the Trinity is a puzzle with no logical solution. Christian doctrines like the Trinity are meant to awaken the Christian to what is beyond the mind. It is not meant to convey information about God, but to lead to a direct encounter with God.

Another such doctrine is the Incarnation. The Church spent much of the first four centuries of the Christian era trying to formulate a Christology that would explain the nature of Christ. In fact the question "Who is Christ?" is just another form of the inquiry "Who is God?" The difference is that the Incarnation combines both the "from below" and the "from above" approaches. Because Christ was a human being, it is an inquiry into human nature. Because Christ is Divine, it also an inquiry into the nature of God. By combining these two approaches, the doctrine of Christ is the most important doctrine in Christianity. Like no other question, it effectively pushes us into God. But this needs to be a personal inquiry and not just a recitation of the Church's answer formulated long ago.

Who is Christ? The Christian answer is that Christ is both God and human – truly God and truly man. From a Hindu point of view, those statements are not contradictory, and therefore there is no theological problem. A yogi would not break a sweat answering that question. In Indian philosophy everything – and everyone - is divine. So there is no problem. Therefore there can be no spiritual breakthrough. The Christological conundrum is not a paradox for those who believe that divine avatars are a dime a dozen. Hindu orthodoxy believes that the Divine comes to earth regularly in human form to show the way to spiritual liberation.

But for the Western mind, the doctrine of Christ is a mind-bender. To say that Christ is both God and man is a paradox because human and divine are mutually exclusive categories. Christian theologians tried to solve the problem rationally. Some said Jesus was half divine and half man. Greek mythology had lots of such hybrids. Others said Jesus was God but only appeared to be human. He left no footprints when he walked the roads of Galilee. Others said Jesus was a man who was adopted by the Heavenly Father and granted divinity as a reward for his obedience. All these approaches were eventually rejected by the Church. Christianity affirmed the paradoxical statement that Christ was both fully God and fully human. But that was impossible. By definition God cannot be man, and man cannot be God. It is blasphemy to equate the two. It was because Jesus claimed to be divine that he was accused of blasphemy by the religious authorities at his trial.

For the Christian - and anyone holding the monotheistic worldview, such as Muslims and Jews - the dual nature of Christ is a "stumbling block," to use biblical language. It is literally a scandal (the Greek word is skandalon.) It is meant to offend. It is meant to shock, to break down one's intellectual resistance until it is seen through. When one transcends the mind and perceives the impossible as true, then Christ is seen as he truly is, and God is seen as He truly is. When one's eyes are opened, the two sides of paradox make perfect sense, even though it cannot be explained in words.

The Problem of Suffering

Other Christian beliefs have this same transformative power as the Trinity and the Incarnation. One of the most powerful of these is theodicy, also known as the problem of suffering or the problem of evil. This is the issue often raised by atheists as an argument against the existence of God. It is the problem confronted by Job during his personal experience of unjust suffering. Theodicy points to two contradictory statements that most theists make about God: that God is both all-powerful and all-loving. If God is all-loving, how can He allow suffering and evil in the world, especially the suffering of the innocent? It was stated in its classic form by the Greek philosopher Epicurus 300 years before the birth of Christianity: "Is God willing to prevent evil, but not able? Then he is not omnipotent. Is he able, but not willing? Then he is malevolent. Is he both able and willing? Then whence cometh evil? Is he neither able nor willing? Then why call him God?"

When the problem of theodicy is investigated honestly one is left with three choices. With the atheist we can conclude that the theistic God does not exist, or if he does exist he is not worthy of worship. This is the response of Job's wife, who advises her husband to "Curse God and die!" (Job 2:9) Second, one can give simplistic religious answers, like the friends of Job and the final editor of the Book of Job, who adds a "happy ending" to this profound book. One can blame suffering on unacknowledged sin (blame the victim). One can blame evil on Satan (the devil made me do it). Or one can attack the questioner as being unfaithful to God for raising the issue.

The third religious answer found in the Book of Job, and often voiced by Christians, is that we must respond to suffering and evil with faith. When all else fails, one can always play the "faith card." Just trust God that there is an answer to the theodical problem, even though one does not see it. Believe that evil is actually good in disguise, that what appears to be evil is really God at work orchestrating everything toward a greater good. Everything is good when viewed from a divine perspective. In this worldview, the torture and death of six million Jews by the Nazis was part of God's good plan. Such an answer borders on the obscene when voiced in the presence of Holocaust survivors.

Of all the religious answers, the most satisfying is a variation on this theme. It is the testimony of the apostle Paul that "All things work together for good to those who love God and are the called according to his purpose." (Romans 8:28) But that variation on the "faith card" still falls short. It does not explain the suffering of those who do not "love God and are called according to his purpose." It tacitly justifies the suffering of those without faith as somehow acceptable. It is really just a variation of the "blame the victim" answer of Job's friends. How about the suffering of infants? What about all the suffering of humanity before God picked the Jews to be his chosen people, or before God sent Christ to be the Savior of the world? Upon close examination, this theological answer to the problem of theodicy also fails to reconcile a genuinely good God with the presence of innocent suffering.

When one makes a thorough inquiry into the problem of theodicy, one confronts the reality that there is no good theological answer. When one sincerely and uncompromisingly investigates the

Christian doctrine of God in the light of evil and suffering, one is pushed beyond all theological answers. Like Job, one is pushed into the Presence of God. In Presence all paradoxes are resolved in Oneness that transcends reason. Then the problem of suffering is seen as another pointer to Truth. When one follows it to God, then the problem of theodicy falls away. In the final chapter of the Book of Job, it says that Job repents. (42:6) The Greek word for repentance is metanoia, which means literally "beyond the mind." When one investigates theological paradox, one goes beyond the mind. There in the eye of the theodical storm is Peace.

Is God Personal or Impersonal?

One recurring question concerning the nature of God is whether God is personal or impersonal. Here we find different answers in East and West. Christianity answers that God is personal – a Heavenly Father known through a personal Savior, Jesus Christ. Hinduism says that God can be conceived of, and worshipped as, personal, but ultimately God is impersonal Absolute. The Divine is understood in the East as impersonal Brahman, which is identical with man's true nature as impersonal atman.

Nondual Christianity answers that God is more than impersonal and more than personal. From a Christian point of view, to say that God is impersonal is to make God less than human. To say that God is personal is to say that God is no more than human. God is more than either philosophy. Meister Eckhart, the fourteenth century German theologian, makes the distinction between God and Godhead. God is personal to persons. God is impersonal to the impersonal. But True God – Godhead - is more than either. If one must use theological words, it is best to say that God is transpersonal or suprapersonal. God is more than is dreamt of in our philosophies, to paraphrase the bard of Avon.

In Christianity this nondual Divinity is given expression in the Holy Spirit. In the Old Testament the Hebrew word for Spirit is feminine. There is a well-known passage in the Book of Proverbs, Chapter 8, which portrays Divine Wisdom as a woman. In the New Testament, the Greek word for Spirit is neuter, and yet it is often coupled with a masculine pronoun. Taken as a whole, the Christian Scriptures embrace all three understandings of the Holy Spirit. This, of course, is impossible from a human point of view. The Holy Spirit refers to a God that includes personal representations (both male and female) and impersonal, and at the same time points beyond the duality of human thought and language to the nonduality that is God's true nature. The Lord our God, the Lord is One.

.

5

THE POWER OF NEGATIVE THINKING

"Emptiness, emptiness, all is emptiness"
– Book of Ecclesiastes

In the Hebrew Scriptures nonduality is most clearly seen in the Wisdom tradition. Of the Wisdom literature, the book that ponders it most deeply is Ecclesiastes. The book opens with the famous words: "Vanity of vanity, all is vanity." This refrain is repeated throughout the book. The Hebrew word traditionally rendered "vanity" is rendered in other translations as meaningless, futility, or pointless. The best translation is emptiness. "Emptiness, emptiness, all is emptiness" The Hebrew word is "hebel." It literally means breath or vapor. It refers to that which is insubstantial, impermanent, or transitory. The

Hebrew word is used more often in Ecclesiastes than all the rest of the Bible combined.

The author of Ecclesiastes, identified in the book simply as "the preacher" or "the teacher" (traditionally identified as King Solomon), proclaims the transient nature of existence. Everything is impermanent, and therefore nothing has eternal substance. The book is an exhaustive examination of every aspect of human life. At the conclusion of each investigation, he pronounces that "this too is emptiness and grasping for the wind." The physical world is seen through. Human nature is seen through.

The Wisdom psalms communicate the same message: "Yes, every mortal man is only a vapor. Certainly, man walks about like a mere shadow." (Psalm 39:5-6, Holman Christian Standard Bible) "Men are only a vapor; exalted men, an illusion. Weighed in the scales, they go up; together they are less than a vapor." (Psalm 62:9, Holman Christian Standard Bible) This word translated "vapor" in these psalms is the same Hebrew word "hebel" – emptiness.

Ecclesiastes declares that the world and man's true nature are emptiness. This has led many people to conclude that Ecclesiastes is a pessimistic book. It has been called a book of existential angst and despair. I recently heard a Christian call it the most depressing book of the Bible. But that is to see it from a modern materialistic point of view. The truth of emptiness proclaimed in Ecclesiastes is not meant to depress the reader. It is intended to point the reader beyond the material and psychological worlds. Emptiness is not bad. It is simply true. And if it is true, how can truth be bad? It just points us beyond what is not real to that which is Real.

The Emptiness of Christ

The apostle Paul wrote: "Let the same mind be in you that was in Christ Jesus, who, though he was in the form of God, did not regard equality with God as something to be exploited, but emptied himself, taking the form of a slave, being born in human likeness. And being found in human form, he humbled himself and became obedient to the point of death — even death on a cross." (Philippians 2:5-8 New Revised Standard Version)

Christian theology refers to this "emptying" by the Greek term "kenosis." It means "to make empty" or "make void." In traditional Christology it describes the Incarnation. To become a human being, the eternal God had to empty himself. It is also used of the Cross. Christ emptied himself – in the sense of humbling himself - to die on a Cross. The corresponding Christian virtue is humility. It is taking the lowest possible position. The Tao Te Ching describes it as the way of water. "The supreme good is like water, which nourishes all things without trying to. It is content with the low places that people disdain. Thus it is like the Tao." (Tao Te Ching, 8)

The Mind of Christ is Emptiness. This is the Mind from which the universe was created. It was spoken into existence by the Mind of Christ. "All things were made through Him, and without Him nothing was made that was made." (John 1:3) Christians are instructed to have this Mind of Christ. In another place, the same apostle tells us that we already have the Mind of Christ. (I Corinthians 2:16) It is just a matter of identifying with, and living from, that Mind. This statement comes at the end of a chapter that describes spiritual seeing, which I would also call nondual seeing. The apostle Paul quotes the Wisdom tradition of the Old Testament several times in this passage. It is worth quoting in its entirety.

"We declare God's wisdom, a mystery that has been hidden and that God destined for our glory before time began. None of the rulers of this age understood it, for if they had, they would not have crucified the Lord of glory. However, as it is written: 'What no eye has seen, what no ear has heard, and what no human mind has conceived' — the things God has prepared for those who love him — these are the things God has revealed to us by his Spirit. The Spirit searches all things, even the deep things of God. For who knows a person's thoughts except their own spirit within them? In the same way no one knows the thoughts of God except the Spirit of God. What we have received is not the spirit of the world, but the Spirit who is from God, so that we may understand what God has freely given us. This is what we speak, not in words taught us by human wisdom but in words taught by the Spirit, explaining spiritual realities with Spirit-taught words. The person without the Spirit does not accept the things that come from the Spirit of God but considers them foolishness, and cannot understand them because they are discerned only through the Spirit. The person with the Spirit makes judgments about all things, but such a person is not subject to merely human judgments, for, 'Who has known the mind of the Lord so as to instruct him?' But we have the mind of Christ." (I Corinthians 2:7-16)

This passage speaks of the incommunicable nature of spiritual awareness. Nondual wisdom cannot be seen with the eye, nor heard with the ear, nor conceived by the human mind. It is communicated directly from Spirit to spirit – from Divine Nature to human nature. It cannot be taught in human words, but only taught by the Spirit. It has no content – and hence it is Empty – and yet this Emptiness holds all things within it. This is the Mind of Christ. We have the Mind of Christ.

Eat, Drink, Chop Wood, Carry Water

According to Ecclesiastes, the human expression of Emptiness is found in ordinariness. A refrain that run throughout the book is that when one realizes the Emptiness at the heart of existence, the result is a return to the ordinary. This is not the emptiness of despair, as conventional commentators interpret the book. This is an awakening to the joyful sacredness of the ordinary.

"Nothing is better for a man than that he should eat and drink, and that his soul should enjoy good in his labor. This also, I saw, was from the hand of God." (Ecclesiastes 2:24) "Every man should eat and drink and enjoy the good of all his labor - it is the gift of God." (Ecclesiastes 3:13) "Here is what I have seen: It is good and fitting for one to eat and drink, and to enjoy the good of all his labor in which he toils under the sun all the days of his life which God gives him; for it is his heritage." (Ecclesiastes 5:18) "So I commended enjoyment, because a man has nothing better under the sun than to eat, drink, and be merry; for this will remain with him in his labor all the days of his life which God gives him under the sun." (Ecclesiastes 8:15) "Go, eat your bread with joy, And drink your wine with a merry heart; For God has already accepted your works." (Ecclesiastes 9:7)

The Zen proverb says, "Before Enlightenment: chop wood, carry water. After enlightenment: chop wood, carry water." Ecclesiastes would say, "Before realizing Emptiness: eat, drink, work. After realizing Emptiness: eat, drink, work." The only difference is that when one awakens to Wisdom, there is abiding joy. Everything is seen as a Gift.

Don't Take Your Self Seriously

Awakening to the true nature of existence reveals the transient nature of the human self. We are nothing more than a wisp of mist disappearing in the breeze of time. This is a common theme in the Wisdom psalms. "My days are like a shadow that lengthens, And I wither away like grass. But You, O Lord, shall endure forever." (Psalm 102:11-12) "As for man, his days are like grass; As a flower of the field, so he flourishes. For the wind passes over it, and it is gone, And its place remembers it no more. But the mercy of the Lord is from everlasting to everlasting." (Psalm 103:15-17)

The Judeo-Christian tradition would not go so far as to say that the human self does not exist. Neither would it say that the world is an illusion. Historians of religion consider traditionally Western religions to be "world-affirming" and "this-worldly" in contrast to the "world-denying" and "other-worldly" character of the Eastern religious traditions. For Christians the world is real, and the human self is real. But they are real only in a relative sense. They are not real in an absolute sense. They have no independent lasting existence apart from God. They exist now only by the command of God spoken into the Void.

Indeed in the Old Testament there is no afterlife for the personal self. The Teacher of Ecclesiastes says, "I said in my heart, 'Concerning the condition of the sons of men, God tests them, that they may see that they themselves are like animals.' For what happens to the sons of men also happens to animals; one thing befalls them: as one dies, so dies the other. Surely, they all have one breath; man has no advantage over animals, for all is vanity. All go to one place: all are from the dust, and all return to dust. Who knows the spirit of the sons of men, which goes upward, and the spirit of the animal, which goes down to the earth? So I perceived that nothing is better than that a man should rejoice in his own works, for that is his heritage." (Ecclesiastes 3:18-22) In the Wisdom tradition humans are temporary phenomena. Wisdom is found in realizing this directly. "Teach us to number our days that we may gain a heart of wisdom." (Psalm 90:12)

In the New Testament, afterlife is clearly taught, but not in the sense that most Christians imagine. Examples of personal souls arriving at the pearly gates, which are so prevalent in Saint Peter jokes and the popular understanding of heaven, are missing from Christian scriptures. Those who inhabit the Biblical scenes of heaven are curiously free of individuality. The people in heaven in Revelation are clearly representative and symbolic.

With the exception of the fictional character of the rich man in Jesus' parable of "Lazarus and the Rich Man," there are no examples in Scripture of identifiable persons in heaven. And with this parable, one must remember that both the rich man and

Lazarus are fictional characters. Even then the fictional Lazarus does not have a speaking part in the story. In fact the character who is most identifiable as an individual in the story is the rich man, and he is in Hades! Ego is hell, and heaven is egolessness!

There are some examples of persons in Scripture who temporarily visit heaven while still alive on earth, such as the narrator of the Book of Revelation. But this is a literary technique, like Dante visiting hell, purgatory and paradise in the Divine Comedy. What John experienced in the Book of Revelation is more akin to a Near Death Experience than an After Death Experience.

Believers certainly do inherit eternal life. Believers do not cease to be at death. That is a clear and consistent teaching of the New Testament. But they leave themselves behind when they enter the Kingdom of Heaven. They must empty their hands of the things of earth, including their earthly selves, in order to receive eternal life.

Eternal life is God's Divine life. People have to leave their human shell behind to enter it. "Flesh and blood cannot inherit the kingdom of God; nor does corruption inherit incorruption." (I Corinthians 15:50) Jesus taught that one can only take as much into the Kingdom of God as will fit through the eye of a needle. That is a poetic way of saying we can take nothing from earthly life into eternal life. That includes the psychological self that we have so laboriously built. We can take with us only what we brought into this world. "For we brought nothing into the world, and we certainly can't carry anything out." (I Timothy 6:7) We did not bring our self into this world, and cannot take our self out.

We survive death, but not in the way we commonly think, because we are not who we think we are. There is eternal life, but the egocentric personality does not inherit it. The self must die for us to live. Then what survives death? The spirit of man in union with the Spirit of God. We survive in Christ.

The individual believer is described by the apostle Paul as being "in Christ," one in Christ, united with Christ. We are no longer separate from Christ. We only live in Christ. "It is no longer I who live, but Christ who lives in me." What survives is our true self in Christ. "But God ... made us alive together with Christ (by grace you have been saved), and raised us up together, and made us sit together in the heavenly places in Christ Jesus." (Ephesians 2:6) Indeed this eternal life was true before our birth. "Blessed be the God and Father of our Lord Jesus Christ, who has blessed us with every spiritual blessing in the heavenly places in Christ, just as He chose us in Him before the foundation of the world, that we should be holy and without blame before Him in love." (Ephesians 1:3-4)

Heaven is a place without suffering. That is also the clear teaching of Scripture. "There shall be no more death, nor sorrow, nor crying. There shall be no more pain, for the former things have passed away." (Revelation 21:4) The source of suffering is the self. It must die for us to live without suffering. Human being is emptied of the human. What remains is Being. Emptiness is filled with the fullness of Christ. This Fullness is eternal life.

Will we be conscious after death? Yes! Consciousness is our true nature. We will be who we truly are now – only freed from the temporal body and psyche. Conscious Joy of Being is eternal life. This is present now. We can enjoy eternal life before physical death. We have Eternal Life now. It is our birthright as children of God.

Will we be reunited with our dearly departed loved ones? Oh my! Of course! In a "re-union" with Christ, a union with God, that is much more intimate than our earthly human relationships can ever be! To have a foretaste of this union now, we just need to not take our selves so seriously.

.

6

THE WAYLESS WAY

"The wayless way is where the sons of God lose themselves
and at the same time find themselves."
- Meister Eckhart

So far this book has been an attempt to describe the nondual Christian experience of God. In this chapter I want to go beyond description and point the reader directly to God. I will make this as personal as I can and describe my own practice of abiding in God. Much of what I say will likely sound obscure. I do not mean to make it so. It is just the nature of language.

I cannot find words to communicate what I want to communicate. I know what I want to say, but I can't say it. The words get tangled up. They contradict each other. As soon as I say one thing, I immediately want to say the opposite in order to clarify the first statement. But that seems to make it even more confusing. Sometimes I think it is futile to even try. But the preacher in me insists that I must make the attempt, even if it is not successful.

God as Wholly Other

My experience of God is that the "I" cannot know God. The "self" dissolves like dew when the Sun shines on it. The personal "I" is darkness, and darkness cannot exist in the Light. The self cannot stand in the Presence of God. God said to Moses, "No one shall see Me, and live." (Exodus 33:20) Where God is, I am not. Where I am, God is not. Therefore "I" cannot experience God, but God is experienced.

I wish I could use another word instead of "experience." That word assumes something is experienced and someone is doing the experiencing. That is not the case. God is not an object to be experienced, and there is no experiencer. The two are one in experiencing. This is nonduality or oneness.

Oneness with God is the open space of wakefulness where experience occurs. Even the word "God" is problematic when talking about this. God is a word that describes a concept in the mind. I am actually speaking about a non-experience by the no-self of that to which the word "God" points. Do you see how difficult it is to communicate this? Such language sounds like gobbledygook. So I am forced to use conventional language, even though I know it will be misunderstood.

In my experience, the best way to know God directly is to explore what is not "I" in my consciousness. This is not as difficult as it may seem. There are many times during the day when the "I" is in the background. Actually whenever one attempts to look at the "I," it freezes like a deer caught in the beam of a car's headlights. It is a vampire-like creature that shrinks from the light of attention. It is a shadowy, ephemeral creature. When one makes a careful inquiry into the nature of the personal self, we can see that the "I" is really around only when we think about it, but not when we look directly at it. We assume the "I" is our real identity, our everyday normal consciousness, but upon examination we see that it is just an occasional actor on the stage of our lives. It thinks it has the starring role in life, but it is just a minor character actor who has an exaggerated sense of his own importance. The leading role goes to God.

By "God" I mean the real conscious Presence which is living our lives. We are not who we think we are. We are not the self. We are the earthen vessel through which the Divine lives life. As the apostle Paul says, "We have this treasure in earthen vessels, that the excellence of the power may be of God and not of us." (2 Corinthians 4:7)

We are nothing but an empty shell. God is everything. God sees through our eyes, and feels through our body, and perceives through our consciousness. As Paul says, "We have the Mind of Christ." (1 Corinthian 2:16) We are instruments of God. God is living his life through us and through the world. The Prayer of Saint Patrick expresses this reality:

Christ with me, Christ before me, Christ behind me,
Christ in me, Christ beneath me, Christ above me,
Christ on my right, Christ on my left,
Christ when I lie down,
Christ when I sit,
Christ when I stand,
Christ in the heart of everyone who thinks of me,
Christ in the mouth of everyone who speaks of me,
Christ in every eye that sees me,
Christ in every ear that hears me.

To know this conscious Presence of God is freedom. It is salvation. The Christian doctrine of the human body as the temple of the Holy Spirit teaches this. "Do you not know that your body is the temple of the Holy Spirit who is in you, whom you have from God, and you are not your own?" (I Corinthians 6:19)

The doctrine of the Church as the Body of Christ teaches this also. We are the physical body of the spiritual Christ. Christ is living his Life through us corporately as well as individually. Once again I will quote my favorite scripture text, "It is no longer I who live but Christ who lives in me." (Galatians 2:20) Our bodies, which include our psychological selves, are simply vessels of God. The "I," the separate self, is just along for the ride. Usually he just gets in the way. We are much better off without him. The True Actor of our lives is the One that we call God.

God is clearly experienced when our attention is directed away from self to that which is "not-self" in our lives. God is so close and so simple that He is overlooked. Augustine says, "God is closer to us that we are to ourselves." All we have to do is turn away from our selves, and there is God! God is literally everywhere in our lives. Even the "I" exists only in God. Everything is filled with God! Everything is God!

Once again I must explain that this is not a philosophical statement of pantheism or monism. I am not speaking theologically or philosophically. I am speaking experientially. Theology does not describe the metaphysical but the experiential. I am describing the way life is perceived. It is perceived as One. This is nonduality. This is Oneness.

To experience God directly all we have to do is step outside of ourselves for a moment. One way to do this is to cease thinking for a moment. Try it now. For ten or fifteen seconds, let your mind rest from any thought. That which is present when there are no thoughts is Presence. It is not the presence of self, but the Presence of God. It is "I am." Not the idea "I am," conceived by the mind, but the simple awareness that I am.

When God described himself to Moses at the burning bush he said, "I am." That "I am-ness" is Eternal God abiding in us and through us, outside us and around us. We normally assume that this sense of "I am" is our personal existence, our psychological self, our individual separate consciousness. But upon inspection it is seen that it is not. We can see that the self exists within this Awareness. This Awareness is God living in us and through us. We are in God. "In Him we live and move and have our being." Everything is in God, and God is living in and through every other part of Creation. The only difference is that in human beings there is consciousness of this Divine Presence.

When we examine this Presence, we notice qualities proceeding from Presence. It is Love. The Scripture says that "God is Love." (I John 4:8) It is Joy. It is Peace. These are not characteristics normally attributed to the individual personal self. These are divine characteristics. These are the qualities that the New Testament calls "the fruit of the Spirit."

Presence is Life. Presence is Light. John said of the Eternal Christ, "In Him was Life and the Life was the Light of men." (John 1:4) "God is Light and in him is no darkness at all." (I John 1:5) Presence is Truth. Jesus said, "I am the Way, the Truth, and the Life."

(John 14:6) Direct experience of Presence is the Way to God. It is the only Way to God because the Way is God.

That is what Jesus meant when he said, "I am the Way, the Truth and the Life. No one comes to the Father but by Me." He was not making a religious endorsement of a particular religion later to be called Christianity. In the Gospel of John Jesus is speaking as the Eternal One, the "I am." He is saying that he is the Wayless Way. Christ is speaking as God and is saying that the only Way to God is through God. The Path is the Goal. The only Way to Transcendent God is through Immanent God, but both are the same God. "I and the Father are One." That is why the early Christian movement was called "the Way" during New Testament times. It is not a religion. It is the Way.

Do not take my word for this. Experience this for yourself. Give attention to this Presence now. Notice the qualities that emanate from Presence. This Presence is not human. It looks nothing like my human self. It is what theologian Rudolf Otto calls "Wholly Other." It is Non-Self.

In Presence is boundless joy. There is more joy than this body or this mind can handle! And the Love! This is not human love. It is nothing like the self-centered, self-absorbed emotion that we call love. This is Divine Unconditional Love.

And the Peace! This is not just happiness. This is the "peace that surpasses all human understanding." (Philippians 4:7) It does not depend on anything happening differently in this life. This Peace is always here. No matter what is happening in our lives, all we have to do is turn in the direction of Presence and Peace floods the soul. This Peace is coming from God. The Joy flows through the body from God. The Love floods the heart. Look for yourself! Is this not God?

Some people say this is not God. They say this is an experience of the human soul, which has been sanctified and beatified by Divine grace. It is a reflection of God in the soul. Perhaps so. The Scriptures say that we are made in the image of God. Perhaps this is the face of God reflected in the mirror of the sanctified soul.

Others call this the "Self" and say that this is our true human nature. These are all different interpretations of the same Reality. Call it whatever you will. I will not squabble over terminology. It does not matter what words are used or how the experience is intellectually processed. These are just words and ideas. I experience this as the Presence of the Holy Spirit. I experience this as what Paul calls "Christ in you, the hope of glory." (Colossians 1:27)

God as Eternal One

Another way to experience God directly is to look outside of time. That is where God dwells. God is Eternal. In Hebrew God is El-Olam, the Everlasting God, the One Who never changes, the eternal One. God is not a time bound creature, and therefore we should not look for God there.

God is not found in the past or the future. But that is exactly where people look for the Divine. We look in the temporal world for evidence of God's existence. This is where atheists think God would be, if there were a God. Of course they do not find him there. Then they conclude that God does not exist. That is like looking for fish in the stratosphere, and when finding none, concluding that fish do not exist. God does not exist in time and space.

Religious people also look for God in the dimensions of time and space, seeking evidence of him in history. They look for Noah's ark on Mount Ararat, the Garden of Eden in Iraq, or the DNA of Jesus on the Shroud of Turin. They seek to prove how Joshua made the sun stand still or how Moses parted the Red Sea. But God is not an historical Figure who can be demonstrated to exist by archeology or historical science. God is beyond time and space. We can know God only beyond time and space.

I invite you to know God now. Do not look for evidence of God in your personal past or seek him in your future. Stop looking for God, and know God now. Some people identify themselves as seekers. That is a sure recipe for failure. People think they will stop seeking when they find God. The truth is just the opposite. We find God only when we stop seeking. "Be still and know that I am God." (Psalm 46:10) Seeking is an activity done in time. To know God we must transcend time.

Past and future are mental conceptions, and God is not a mental conception. Time is relative, and God is absolute. Even scientists now know that time is relative. That was demonstrated by Einstein's Theory of Relativity. Time is flexible. It speeds up and slows down depending on gravity and speed. Time stops when one travels at the speed of light. Time bends like space with gravitational fields. God does not change, and therefore cannot be found in time. The divine is absolute. When we look for the Absolute in the relative, we are looking in the wrong place.

A police officer saw a drunken man intently searching the ground under a lamppost and asked him what he is looking for. The drunk replied that he is looking for his car keys. The officer helped him search for a few minutes without success. Then he asked whether the man is certain that he dropped the keys near the lamppost. "No," was the reply, "I lost the keys somewhere across the street." "Then why are you looking here?" asks the surprised and irritated officer. "The light is better here," the intoxicated man responds with aplomb.

This is the way people search for God and Truth. We look for God in time and space because it is all we know. Where else would we look? But if we are going to find God, we must look outside of time. God is only found now. This is where the Scriptures point us. The apostle Paul says, "Now is the accepted time; behold, now is the day of salvation." (2 Corinthians 6:2) Jesus said, "Do not worry about tomorrow, for tomorrow will worry about itself." (Matthew 6:34) "Today, if you will hear His voice, Do not harden your hearts." (Hebrews 4:7) In the New Testament the Day of Salvation is always today. Yesterday is too late and tomorrow never comes. The Kingdom of God is now. This is why I call God Presence. Presence is only in the present.

How do we look in the Present? It is quite simple. Look beyond thought. Take a moment to watch your thoughts. Do not follow them or become lost in them. Just watch them go by. When you catch yourself being carried away by thought, notice that also. That is also a thought. Watch that thought also. Notice that nearly every thought is about the past or the future. That is where our mind spends most of its time, but that is not where you will find God.

Usually thoughts carry with them emotions concerning the past or the future, often very strong emotions. They carry with them desire or repulsion, mental pain or pleasure. Notice the emotions. Notice that ideas about the past and future are just ideas.

There is no need to get emotional. They are ideas in your head. They are not really happening. They do not exist except in your mind. They are nothing more than ideas.

Now notice the Space in which ideas form. Feel the quality of the Space. It is peace and quiet. It is always peace and quiet, regardless of how troublesome those thoughts are. That Space is the Kingdom of God. That is where God dwells. That is the Presence of God. It is always the Present, and God is always here now. Sometimes people stumble upon the Kingdom of God. Jesus told stories about such people, such as the man who expectedly found a treasure in a field that he was plowing. Other people purposefully search for it, like in Jesus' story of the merchant who searched all his life for the Pearl of Great Price.

Some people find the Present in "extreme sports." Death-defying activities force people to focus on the Present. Their lives depend on paying complete attention to what is happening right now. If they stop paying attention for a moment, they are dead. They report feeling like time slows down or even stops. They are no longer conscious of themselves. There is just pure awakeness. People are willing to risk their lives repeatedly in order to experience this state. Nondual spirituality is like an extreme sport. It is done in the Now. Our Eternal Life depends on it. That is the only place that Eternal Life is found – in the Eternity of the Present.

We can abide in this Eternal Now always. It is where we always are anyway. All we have to do is notice it. If we let go of thoughts of past and future, we find ourselves naturally Present. It happens naturally because this is where already are. We are always Here Now. We overlook that Reality by directing our attention to everywhen but now.

Janus, the Greek god of time, is pictured as two-faced – one face looking back to the past and one forward to the future. We are children of Janus. We are always looking backwards or forwards. God lives in the space between our two temporal faces. Mental and emotional suffering comes from living where God is not - in the past and the future. When we live in the Present, suffering stops and Eternal Living begins.

We discover the same divine qualities in the Present that we experienced in the Not-self. Perhaps we should call the Present Not-time. Our minds can easily turn the present into another concept. We are so brainwashed by time that we view the Present as a very brief period of time. But the Present is not time. It is not a second or a nanosecond. It is Timeless. It is Eternity. It is the Kingdom of Heaven. It is the Second Coming of Christ. Christ comes not in time, but in Eternity. Christ is now. Christ never left. He has always been here. "I will be with you always." (Matthew 28:20)

When we live Now, time ceases and eternity appears. The veil of time is pulled back to reveal the One who is always here and never in time. We come face to face with God. It takes no time at all to awake to this Eternal Presence. There is no journey to make. There is no path to follow. Christ is now. He is the Wayless Way, which is the only Way. Jesus said, "Abide in Me, and I in you." (John 15:4) Then the past and the present collapse into One. The two become one in Christ, the Eternal One.

EPILOGUE

The Story of Me

My personal story is the least important part of this book. But some readers may find it helpful to hear the story of how a Baptist preacher came to experience God in a decidedly nonbaptist way. So I include it here in its proper place at the end. I will limit my statements to my spiritual journey, since other biographical information is of little significance.

My first awareness of the reality of the Spirit occurred when I was 13 years old. I had been going through confirmation classes at the local Congregational church. Perhaps that is why God was on my mind, and why I called out to God when I felt desperate. My adolescent crisis consisted of being prevented from attending the highlight of the school year - the end-of-year eighth grade outing to the beach.

The reason was a fever. The doctor said I could only attend if my fever broke. I prayed fervently for healing, promising God all sorts of important things (which I have long since forgotten.) I received the desired healing and romped at the seaside in my new swimming trunks. This would not be considered a miracle by Vatican standards, but to my young mind it was proof that God was real and answered prayers.

In typical teenage fashion I quickly forgot God's grace. In the years that followed I went from this simple childhood faith to atheistic existentialism. My high school years were filled with books by Camus, Sartre, and Nietzsche – heavy reading for a teen. By the time I entered college I was an atheist, and I eagerly enrolled in Religion 101 during my freshman year to defend my unbelief. It was 1968 and the topic for the semester was the Death of God movement.

Strangely enough, reading about the demise of God only made me more interested in religion. I took more courses offered by the Religion department. Before long I had switched my major from Geology to Religion, to the bewilderment of my academic advisor, who was also the head of the Geology department. The reason I gave for my decision was that I needed something "more practical" than science. He shook his head in perplexity.

My academic study of religion led me to read widely and deeply in all the faiths of the world's peoples. I began to explore the world's religions with a personal interest as well as academic curiosity. I was especially attracted to the mystical expressions of religion. I discovered the Christian mystics and did a semester-long independent study of the fourteenth century German mystic, Meister Eckhart. At the same time I was studying Eastern texts, such as the Tao Te Ching, the Bhagavad Gita, and the Upanishads.

My personal spiritual search lasted about four years during the late 1960's and early 70's. One day, after an exhaustive intellectual and inner quest, I found myself alone in my 1967 Ford Fairlaine, parked at the ocean on my lunch break, with a paperback New Testament in my hands. With a winter storm battering the coast of Salem, Massachusetts, I prayerfully gave my life to Jesus Christ. I was, to use the term in vogue among evangelicals, born again. A few months later I was baptized in that same ocean by the pastor of a nearby Baptist church.

Never being one to do anything halfway, I threw all my energy into being a disciple of Christ.

Within a year of my conversion, I entered seminary, which I viewed as an intensive course in personal spiritual development. My career plan was to become a university or seminary professor, teaching World Religions from a Christian perspective.

Between earning my Masters degree and my Doctorate, I decided to take a break from academia for a year or two and serve as pastor of a church. I had ministered as a part-time pastor during seminary and viewed parish ministry as a temporary reprieve from the rigors of graduate school. I also hoped to raise a little money for tuition. I quickly discovered that I loved being a fulltime pastor. That was 1978, and I have been a pastor ever since.

During these years of professional ministry, I have considered myself a traditional Christian in doctrine and ethics. At some points during my ministry, I was more conservative and at other times more moderate. But I have always placed myself squarely in the Christian camp. Then four years ago, something changed. Perhaps I should say that something stopped ... or began to stop. I began to stop. My persona – the personal self - with all its beliefs began to unravel.

As I look back on it, I see signs of this process earlier in my spiritual journey. Shortly after my conversion, I had an encounter with the Divine that rocked me to the core. I described it to my fiancée at that time (now my wife of 40 years) as God brushing me with his finger. It felt as if I was dissolving. I cried out like the prophet Isaiah, "Woe is me! I am undone! For I have seen the Lord!" I physically trembled in the presence of God.

Twenty years later I had an even stronger experience. I had been taking a yearlong program for spiritual directors at the Shalem Institute for Spiritual Formation in Washington, DC. I was participating in a weeklong silent retreat. During one session of group contemplative prayer, I had the overwhelming sense that I was dying. I knew intellectually that I was not physically dying, but I felt like I was psychologically dying. My psyche was crumbling. My sense of a separate self was dissolving, and it was terrifying. My emotional response to this experience of nonbeing was "fear and trembling." I thought I was losing my mind. That assessment was not far wrong.

Unfortunately the leaders in charge of the retreat did not know what was happening to me, and they could not counsel me through it. I returned home early from the retreat, and consulted my spiritual director. She also did not know how to help me. She consulted her fellow spiritual directors for guidance. Slowly, with her help, I worked through what had happened to me in Washington.

Over time I somewhat accommodated this sense of diminished self as my "new reality," but for the most part I resisted it and suppressed it. I did not successfully integrate this experience into my Christian faith. I eventually rejected the practice of contemplative spirituality as a psychologically dangerous path for me. I threw myself back into evangelical Christianity with renewed fervor.

I considered the church I was serving in New Hampshire to be too liberal for my renewed evangelicalism. I moved to Calvary Baptist Church in Lowell, Massachusetts. After a few years there I found an even more conservative church in Rochester, Pennsylvania. At the First Baptist Church of Rochester, I established my conservative evangelical credentials in church, community and denomination. The church was thriving, but the denominational ethos was too liberal for me.

The church eventually left the American Baptist denomination and joined the Southern Baptist Convention. During this period I wrote a book entitled "More Than a Purpose," (published in 2006) which challenged the evangelical credentials of the bestselling "The Purpose Driven Life" and the wider megachurch movement. Even the popular evangelical pastor Rick Warren was not conservative enough for me!

But my religious fervor had its price. Interpersonal conflict with church members, clergy and the denomination took its toll on me. Even though I had the support of a large majority of my congregation, I was emotionally wounded by the experience of church conflict. Suffering from depression, I left the ministry in 2009, thinking that my departure from Christian ministry was permanent. It turned out to be a one-and-a half year hiatus.

When I resigned my position as a pastor, something changed in me. I was spiritually and psychologically devastated. I described it to a Southern Baptist colleague at the time as Spiritual Post Traumatic Stress. But it turns out that this was a good development. It is exactly what needed to happen. God was breaking the shell of my self.

With my resignation from fulltime ministry came an identity crisis. I wondered: If I am no longer a pastor, then who am I? I had always been a professional church leader. I was the Reverend Doctor. Since my early days in the Jesus movement in the 1970's, I had been an evangelical spiritual leader. Who was I now?

This prompted an intense inquiry into my personal identity. Who was I beneath my titles, degrees and roles? Who is God beneath his titles and roles? What did I really know to be true? I questioned everything about my Christian faith, delving down to its very foundation.

Nothing was too sacred to doubt. My search for deeper truth took me into a renewed study of atheism. I read dozens of books by the New Atheists and old atheists. Reading these authors with an open mind challenged my understanding of God.

I found myself agreeing with much of what the atheists wrote. I came to see that the traditional deity of Western culture did not exist. Yet at the same time, I was gradually becoming aware of God beyond labels, ideas, theologies and religions.

While I was questioning the nature of God, I also questioned my understanding of my own self. I studied the atheist understanding of human nature as a purely evolutionary animal. Once again I came to accept much of what the atheists said.

At the same time I became more conscious of who I was beyond the human animal. In short, there gradually appeared – and continues to appear - a direct knowing of myself and God apart from mental conceptions. This has happened gradually over the last four years, but more fully within the last year.

It was accelerated by a physician's misdiagnosis. A doctor solemnly informed me that I had pancreatic cancer. For one week in 2012, I was dying. Then a further test revealed that I did not have cancer after all. But for seven days, I emotionally came to terms with my imminent death. It was traumatic for both my wife and I at the time. Now looking back, I see it as a blessing. It made me look into my mortality with an intensity that I could never have mustered without the doctor's prognosis.

I do not know exactly how to describe this new awareness of myself and God. Words are inadequate, and even ideas fail to capture it. It is a sense of Oneness. God is perceived as Real, but not as an entity separate from me. God is not seen an entity at all; neither do I experience myself in this way. Meister Eckhart wrote: "The eye with which I see God is the same eye with which God sees me." Seeing one is seeing the other. In seeing who I am, I see who God is.

Jesus expressed his experience saying, "I and the Father are one. When you have seen me you have seen the Father." Somehow I intuitively understand Christ's awareness. "Have this mind in you which was also in Christ Jesus," the apostle Paul said. Elsewhere he wrote, "It is no longer I who live but Christ who lives in me." I am not; Christ is.

"We have this treasure in earthen vessels,' Paul says. There is this earthen vessel of a body. There is this consciousness of the body, called the self. But I am neither of these. I never really was. There is just God, the Treasure in earthen vessels.

The clearest way I can describe it is this: my sense of being a separate self has been diminished. It is not gone. Marshall Davis is still here, but it is not me. It is a mask I wear, a role I play. My persona is still real in a temporary sense, but not in an eternal sense. It did not exist before this body was born. It developed in early childhood. It has been changing and growing during my lifetime, and it will cease to exist when the body dies.

But who I really am cannot die. In this sense I was never born and will not die. Jesus said of his experience, "Before Abraham was, I am." The words of Paul also come to mind. "In Him we live and move and have our being."

I am still a Christian. In fact Christ is more real to me than ever before, because my Christianity is based not on blind faith but on faithful sight. Knowing the Oneness of God has deepened my understanding of Christianity. My love for, and devotion, to Christ is stronger. Christ is Lord. He is the Way, the Truth and the Life. My theology remains as Christian as ever. I feel no need to revamp my beliefs to reflect some generic philosophical monism.

In the end all spiritual philosophies are only ideas. They cannot contain God. At best they point beyond themselves to the One who cannot be contained by mental images. Religions are by nature idolatries, replacing God with graven images, even if those images are graven only in the mind. Nondual Christianity points beyond all theology to Reality. As Jesus said, "Abide in Me and I in you." This is where I live.

As far as my professional ministry is concerned, I returned to parish ministry in January of 2011, and I am presently the pastor of the Community Church of Sandwich, New Hampshire. This is the same church I left in 1994 to explore more conservative forms of Christianity. I am back at the same congregation, having come to appreciate the

ecumenicity and spiritual openness of this rural
community church.

.

ABOUT THE AUTHOR

Marshall Davis lives in a small New Hampshire village where he enjoys the mountains and lakes. He is a husband, father, grandfather, cribbage and backgammon player, tea drinker, wood stove feeder, vegetable gardener, walker, occasional hiker, nature lover, and Baptist minister. Along the way he has earned some theological degrees, served as a full-time pastor for forty years, and authored eleven books. But in the end titles, degrees, labels and credentials do not matter ... unless they encourage you to read his books.

BOOKS BY MARSHALL DAVIS

Thank God for Atheists: What Christians Can Learn from the New Atheism

Experiencing God Directly: The Way of Christian Nonduality

The Tao of Christ: A Christian Version of the Tao Te Ching

Living Presence: A Guide to Everyday Awareness of God

More Than a Purpose: An Evangelical Response to Rick Warren and the Megachurch Movement

The Baptist Church Covenant: Its History and Meaning

A People Called Baptist: An Introduction to Baptist History & Heritage

The Practice of the Presence of God in Modern English by Brother Lawrence, translated by Marshall Davis

The Gospel of Solomon: The Christian Message in the Song of Solomon

Esther

The Hidden Ones

Visit Marshall Davis' Author page on Amazon to see a description of these books.

Printed in Great Britain
by Amazon